T0193642

The Sky is the Limit Little Ones?

Mina Z. Atcha and Khadija A. Atcha

Balboa Press books may be ordered through booksellers or by contacting:

Balboa Press
A Division of Hay House
1663 Liberty Drive
Bloomington, IN 47403
www.balboapress.com.au
AU TFN: 1 800 844 925 (Toll Free inside Australia)
AU Local: 0283 107 086 (+61 2 8310 7086 from outside Australia)

ISBN: 978-1-5043-2262-1 (sc)
ISBN: 978-1-5043-2261-4 (e)

Print information available on the last page.

Balboa Press rev. date: 09/26/2020

Fear nothing little ones, you are the bravest

Fear is not silly...
well done!

Beware little one,
a father's trust in
you for good.

Watch out little ones? Thank you!

You know what to do?

My heart is your heart always…

Caution little one...

Beware...

Be careful little one...

Beware...your dog' is
a mammal just like
you and me...

Be careful little one...
Because I love you too much.

Free hug day.

alth Club

Be cautious,
lost property.

Be careful little

Be careful little

You are the greatest daughter ever.

SPOT.

A FATHER'S UNCONDITIONAL LOVE FOR HER

His Daughter's Kindness is her Father's Gratitude;

His Daughter's Laughter is her Father's Joy;

His Daughter's Beauty is her Father's Pride;

His Daughter's Gentle Touch is her Father's Hope;

His Daughter's Sadness is her Father's Tears;

His Daughter's Happiness is her Father's Certainty;

His Daughter's Smile is her Father's Relief;

His Daughter's Anger is her Father's Patience;

His Daughter's Words is her Father's Wisdom;

His Daughters Success is her Fathers Pride;

His Daughter's Honesty is her Father's Promise;

His Daughter's Unconditional Love is her Father's
Unconditional Trust in her;

His Daughter's Heart is her Father's Heart Forever.

Adam S. Atcha

Printed in the United States
By Bookmasters